North York Moors and Coast

Souvenir Book

compiled by Andrew Gallon

Dalesman

First published in 2013 by Dalesman
an imprint of Country Publications Ltd
The Water Mill, Broughton Hall
Skipton
North Yorkshire
BD23 3AG

www.dalesman.co.uk

© Dalesman 2013
Photographs © individual photographers as listed on page 64

Cover:

ISBN 978-1-85568-311-2

All rights reserved. This book must not be circulated in any form of binding or cover other than that in which it is published and without similar condition of this being imposed on the subsequent purchaser. No part of this publication may be reproduced, stored on a retrieval system or transmitted in any form, or by any means, electronic, mechanical, photocopying, recording or otherwise, without either prior permission in writing from the publisher or a licence permitting restricted copying. In the United Kingdom such licences are issued by the Copyright Licensing Agency, 90 Tottenham Court Road, London, W1P 9HE. The right of Dalesman to be identified as author of this work has been asserted by it in accordance with Copyright Designs and Patents Acts 1988.

Printed in China by 1010 Printing

Designed by Black Dog Industries

For sheer variety, the North York Moors and Coast are hard to beat. They offer the visitor a bit of everything. Embark on a voyage of discovery across this beautiful region and you'll find lonely moorland tracts, tranquil dales, stunning coastal scenery, handsome resorts, pretty villages, colourful harbours, breathtaking ecclesiastical ruins, ancient standing stones and burial mounds, the world's most popular heritage steam railway, and bewitching rivers, streams and waterfalls.

Britain's leading photographers have painstakingly captured the very best of the North York Moors and Coast, and we've brought their outstanding work together in this handy pictorial souvenir. The area covered is based roughly on the North York Moors National Park, which celebrated its sixtieth anniversary in 2012. The images that follow are sure to provide a fresh perspective on something you've seen and inspire an expedition somewhere new next time you visit.

Rise and shine

Left: The Robin Hood's Bay coastline is a favourite location for photographers hoping to capture the glorious colours of daybreak. This vantage point is Boggle Hole, with the lens pointing towards the Ravenscar promontory.

Top Right: The breathtaking hues of first light ignite Scarborough's South Bay, with the town's ruinous medieval castle visible on its headland.

Bottom Right: Dawn reflections on the rocky shore of Saltwick Bay.

Falling in love

Left: Mallyan Spout, secreted in a sylvan gorge far below the honeypot village of Goathland, drops 70 feet (18m) into the foaming waters of West Beck.

Middle: Late winter at Hayburn Wyke, where Hayburn Beck, having tumbled through thick woods, decants directly onto the beach as a twin outpouring. Wyke derives from a Scandinavian word for bay.

Right: The Eller Beck's finest moment: Thomason Foss, a short distance upstream from the hamlet of Beck Hole, and its delightfully mossy plunge-pool.

Dream topping

Roseberry Topping, which rises 1,050 feet (320m) above the Cleveland Plain, is one of the North York Moors' most distinctive summits. There is more than one explanation for its Matterhorn-style profile. Some say it's down to Man, others to Nature, though the hill's magnificence, in all seasons, is beyond debate.

Left: Spring, a perspective of Roseberry Topping, looking north from the pond at Aireyholme Farm.

Middle: Summer, from Gribdale, with the heather in full bloom.

Top Right: Autumn, looking across fields to the south of Roseberry Topping.

Bottom Right: Winter, Roseberry from Nunthorpe Church on a frosty morning.

Religious order

Left: Cistercian monks founded Byland Abbey in 1177 and built the structure in the early Gothic style. Impressive surviving aspects include the striking west front, with its ruined great rose window, said to have inspired the rose window in York Minster's south transept.

Right: Gisborough Priory's signature feature is its 97-foot (30m) eastern gable, a key element in this wintry view of the ruinous Augustinian house. One of the Bruce family – a clan later to occupy the Scottish throne – founded the priory in 1119.

Religious order

Left: The east end of Whitby Abbey, silhouetted against the setting sun. The abbey, positioned in a windswept location on cliffs high above the town, dates from the early thirteenth century and was home to Benedictine monks.

Top Right: Inside the atmospheric remains of the presbytery at Rievaulx Abbey, a Cistercian foundation close to the River Rye. The vast wealth generated by the monks who lived and worked here is reflected in the magnitude of the abbey's buildings.

Bottom Right: Mount Grace Priory, near the pretty village of Osmotherley, is the most important Carthusian ruin in England. Its hermit-like monks lived in individual cells. The priory is noted for superb springtime displays of daffodils.

Going loco

Top Left: A driver's view of a 1918 vintage Q6 freight locomotive footplate in the sidings at Grosmont engine shed, the North Yorkshire Moors Railway's busy hub.

Top Middle: The 24-mile (39km) North Yorkshire Moors Railway, which negotiates stunning scenery between Whitby, Grosmont and Pickering, is the world's most popular heritage line. Gresley A4 Pacific Bittern, a sister locomotive of the record-breaking Mallard, coasts downgrade through lonely Newton Dale.

Top Right: A plume of steam betrays just how hard 4MT locomotive the Green Knight is working with a southbound train on the 1-in-49 gradient at Darnholm.

Bottom: Powerful 9F locomotive Cock o' the North makes light of the steady climb along the floor of remote North Dale with a service bound for Whitby.

Nature's bounty

Left: Tranquil Gormire Lake formed in a glacial meltwater channel above the Vale of York. The only natural lake in the North York Moors National Park, it is secreted amid dense woodland and backed by the sheer Whitestone Cliff.

Right: The Pepper Pot, the best known of the Bridestones, an exposed moor-top collection of sandstone rocks which over 150 million years have been caressed and cajoled by the elements into weird and wonderful shapes.

Nature's bounty

Top Left: The setting sun picks out 'ice sculptures' on a snowbound Huntcliff. This exposed Saltburn location was the site of Roman signalling station.

Bottom Left: The cliff-top footpath at Dungeon Hole, part of the 110-mile (177km) Cleveland Way national trail, offers a grandstand view of Robin Hood's Bay and Bay Town – though we cannot guarantee you'll get lighting as dramatic as this.

Right: Autumnal reflections in Staindale Lake, an attractive sheet of water hidden amid the 8,000 sprawling acres (3,237ha) of Dalby Forest. The lake provides a refuge for ducks and geese. Staindale is from a Viking word for stony valley.

Nature's bounty

Left: Legend suggests a giant, Wade, scooped out the Hole of Horcum during a tantrum. The more prosaic truth is that underground springs destabilising limestone layers were responsible for this remarkable 400-foot (122m) deep basin, penetrated by footpaths and the infant Levisham Beck, and next to the A169.

Right: Heather in radiant summer finery cradles peat bog on Egton High Moor.

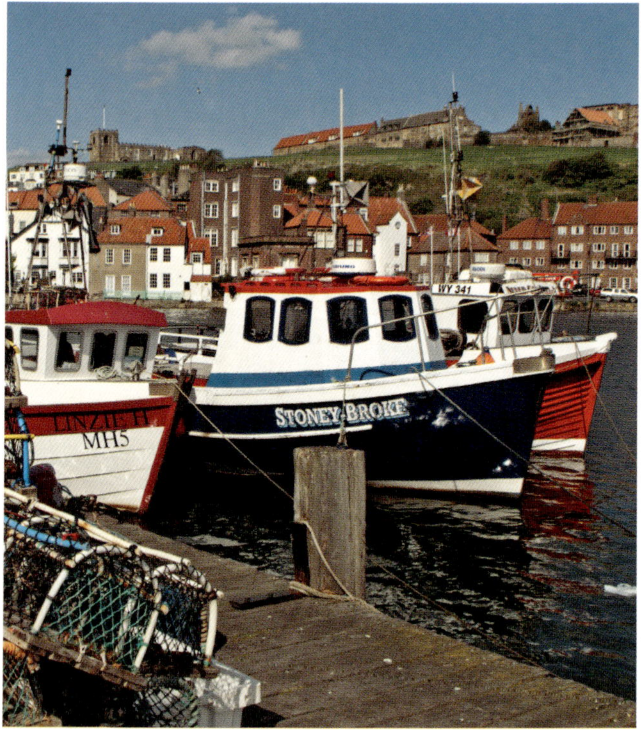
STONEY BROKE
LINZI H
MH5
WY 341

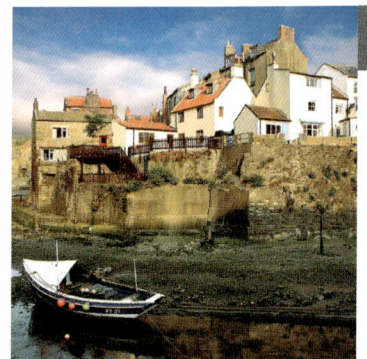

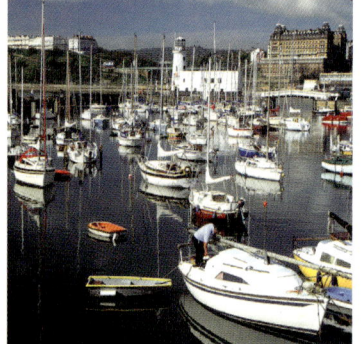

Pass the port

Left: Whitby's upper harbour, beyond the Esk swing bridge, is a fascinating place to wander. Brightly painted fishing boats, surrounded by the equally gaudy paraphernalia of the trade, await their next call to sea.

Top Middle: A tranquil moment in the natural harbour of Staithes, where Roxby Beck empties into the North Sea. This iconic village is one of several North Yorkshire communities associated with Captain James Cook, the great explorer.

Bottom Middle: Leisure craft dominate this view of a packed outer harbour in Scarborough's South Bay. The elegant building to the right of the lighthouse is the Grand, one of the resort's lavish Victorian-era hotels.

Right: Idle fishing boats, drawn up out of harm's way, at Runswick Bay. The cottages which make up this captivating village provide a pleasant backdrop.

Pass the port

Left: This weather-beaten fisherman's hut at Port Mulgrave has seen better days, but doubtless still serves its purpose.

Right: Trawlers, lit dramatically by early-morning sun, rock gently at their moorings alongside the quay in Whitby's picturesque lower harbour.

Village life

Left: The astonishingly compact village of Staithes, seen from the rocky heights of Cowbar Nab. It is one of two headlands which together form a natural harbour, a rarity on this notoriously treacherous coast.

Right: Heartbeat's wheeler-dealer Claude Greengrass probably imagined there was a crock of gold to be unearthed in Goathland, which doubled as Aidensfield in the long-running TV series. Wonder if the loot is at this rainbow's end?

Village life

Above: Hutton-le-Hole, arguably the prettiest village in the North York Moors National Park, hides some of its charms beneath a blanket of snow. There's no mistaking Hutton Beck, however.

Below Left: The moorland village of Lockton is renowned for the floral displays in its cottage gardens, perfectly illustrated in this image taken in high summer.

Below Middle: Pretty Lastingham is noted primarily for its church, visible in this shot, which stands on or near the site of a seventh-century Celtic monastery.

Below Right: The River Leven threads a watery path through the heart of Great Ayton; its grassy banks are a lovely place to linger on summer evenings.

Village life

Below: Castleton, the largest community in upper Esk Dale, boasts a main street built atop a windy ridge.

Right: The banks of the River Seven as it flows dreamily through Sinnington are a hotspot for daffodils in spring, and the blooms attract countless admirers to the village.

After dark

Left: The full length of Saltburn's 120-foot (37m) funicular — the oldest working example in Britain — and 1,500-foot (457m) pier, two of the resort's most remarkable Victorian artefacts, form key elements in this spectacular light show.

Top Right: Looking up the Esk estuary towards Whitby's swing bridge and upper harbour. Bridge and river divide the old and new parts of the town.

Bottom Right: Christmas lights in Thirsk's cobbled market place. The ornate clock tower commemorates the 1896 marriage of the Duke of York.

The light fantastic

Left: Ethereal December mist swirls around Hood Hill at Sutton Bank, where the Hambleton Hills rear dramatically from the pancake-flat Vale of York.

Top Middle: Pickering Low Mill, a Grade II listed structure dating from the early nineteenth century, captured on a bright, frosty Christmas morning. The watercourse is Pickering Beck.

Bottom Middle: Seen from a point halfway down Whitby's famous 199 Steps, which link old town and abbey, the midsummer sun sets spectacularly over the North Sea

Right: As it sinks closer to the western horizon, the January afternoon sun illuminates pockets of Rosedale, once an important ironstone mining centre.

Sun, sea and sand

Left: Scarborough's majestic South Bay and castle-topped promontory seen at their best in a superb spring panorama across the water-grooved sands.

Middle: The Crescent, all elegant Georgian architecture and dazzling flowerbeds, is one of the most alluring parts of Filey, a wholly unspoiled resort retaining a magnetic appeal for visitors.

Right: Colourful wooden bathing huts illuminate the seafront at Whitby and echo the fashion of bygone days.

Life's a beach

Right: Delicate fluting of the sand makes delightful patterns at Robin Hood's Bay, a great spot for rock-pooling. The Ravenscar headland fills the horizon.

Below Left: Groynes, designed to prevent longshore drift, always look more appealing when in a state of disrepair. This classic example is on the beach at Sandsend.

Below Right: Low tide at Boggle Hole. The cliffs on this superb stretch of Yorkshire's Heritage Coast are terribly unstable and require constant vigilance.

Far Right: A lone surfer dreams of the big wave as he heads across Saltburn sands towards the breakers. The resort is widely regarded as a surfers' paradise.

Up dale and down dale

Left: Brrrr! A chilly winter's day in the Vale of York near Coxwold. Sharp eyes will spot the White Horse of Kilburn, on Roulston Scar, sneaking into the picture.

Top Right: The gritters have done a grand job clearing the road that drops steeply off Blakey Ridge towards the Farndale hamlet of Church Houses.

Bottom Right: Castleton Rigg separates Westerdale from Danby Dale. Signs of harvesting are evident in this evening view from the ridge of Westerdale.

Up dale and down dale

Left: Glorious summer weather in lower Bilsdale, with the unmistakable outline of Easterside Hill the highlight of this delightful scene.

Below: Bransdale, one of the least-visited valleys in the North York Moors National Park, looks sublime in autumn regalia. The dale is in the care of the National Trust.

Right: Shafts of sunlight enliven an autumn afternoon in Danby Dale.

Reach for the sky

Left: Walkers on Westerdale Moor take a well-earned break beneath Ralph's Cross, official symbol of the North York Moors National Park.

Middle: The Captain Cook Monument, on Easby Moor, commemorates the legendary explorer who grew up on a farm nearby. Funded by a benefactor from Whitby, the obelisk was erected in 1827. A plaque details Cook's many achievements.

Right: Early morning on Whitby's west pier and a dramatic view of the two 'old' lighthouses guarding the harbour entrance. The light in the foreground was built in 1831, with the other following twenty-three years later.

River dance

The Esk is the foremost river in the North York Moors National Park. Noted for spawning salmon, it rises on Westerdale Moor and flows through 28 varied miles (45km), passing several delightful villages, to reach the North Sea at Whitby. The Esk is tidal as far west as Ruswarp.

Top Left: Sections of the river near Egton Bridge are thickly wooded.

Bottom Left: Lealholm is the prettiest of the villages visited by the River Esk. You can cross the river here on stepping stones.

Right: Hunter's Sty packhorse bridge, dating from medieval times, carries a track over the River Esk near Westerdale village. The bridge was restored in 1874.

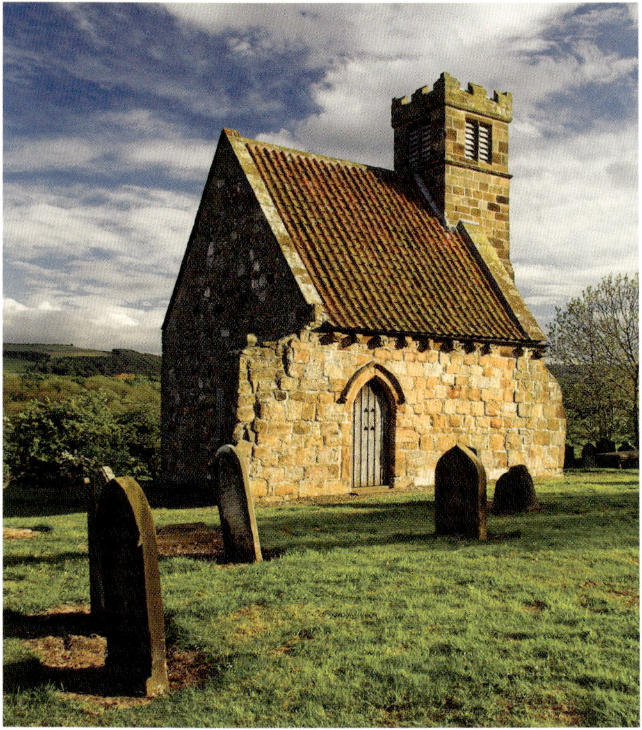

Charmed by churches

Far Left: Upleatham Old Church is one of the smallest in England. Dedicated to St Andrew, its bijou interior is said to measure just 20 feet (6m) by 13 feet (4m).

Left: The spire of St Peter & St Paul's Church dominates Pickering. No visitor should leave this bustling market town without viewing the fifteenth-century paintings adorning the church's plastered interior walls. Part of their function was to help the illiterate understand the Bible's teachings.

Top Right: Daffodils to die for in the graveyard of the Norman Parish Church of St Mary, Over Silton. Originally, the church was dedicated to All Saints.

Bottom Right: The nave of the Parish Church of St Martin-on-the-Hill, on Scarborough's South Cliff. The structure was designed by a youthful George Frederick Bodley, later to become a distinguished Victorian architect, and was built in the early 1860s to serve a wealthy new suburb of Scarborough.

Bays of plenty

Top left: An unusual perspective of Robin Hood's Bay from the grounds of the Raven Hall Hotel in Ravenscar, dubbed since the early 1900s 'the town that never was'. Before a Victorian entrepreneur came along, with bold plans to develop a resort to rival nearby Scarborough, the village was called Peak.

Bottom left: Port Mulgrave, once a busy industrial centre for the mining and shipment of ironstone, is a peaceful spot attracting few visitors. Rosedale Cliffs tower over the sparse remnants of the harbour, formerly a hive of activity.

Right: There's a storm brewing over Runswick Bay, where fishing and leisure boats are dragged up the beach and moored yards beyond the high-water line.

The colour purple

For a short time in summer, the North York Moors don a vivid purple cloak and are transformed into a spectacle that lives long in the memory of visitors.

Left: Striking contrasts in bonny Baysdale, one of the quieter valleys incising the flanks of the North York Moors. A farm in the dale is built on the site of a twelfth-century Cistercian nunnery.

Top: Amid an ocean of heather, Fat Betty, one of the best-known standing stones on the North York Moors, is a striking sight. It is also known as White Cross, with the origin of both names owing much to colourful legends.

Bottom: Mellow evening light catches the heather above Rosedale.

It's show time

Two lovely moments at Ryedale Show: **Left,** a couple of regulars catch up on the latest gossip; and **right,** an owner gives her horse some quiet encouragement. Held for almost 150 years at Welburn Park, Kirkbymoorside, this traditional agricultural show attracts about 15,000 spectators.

Top Middle: Meticulous judges literally weigh up the merits of entries at the Egton Bridge Gooseberry Show, Staged by the Egton Bridge Old Gooseberry Society, the event has been held since 1800 on the first Tuesday in August, and is Britain's longest surviving gooseberry show.

Bottom Middle: Posing amiably for the camera is an impressive entry in one of the cattle classes at Stokesley Show, staged each September since 1859 by the town's agricultural society.

Bridging the gap

Far left: The quiet banks of the River Leven provide Stokesley's most intimate corners, never more endearing than in the "season of mists and mellow fruitfulness".

Middle: Bridges come in all shapes and sizes: this charming example for pedestrians crosses Borough Beck in the heart of Helmsley.

Right: Spa Bridge opened in 1827 and has become an iconic Scarborough landmark. It is 75 feet (23m) high and 414 feet (126m) long. Until the 1950s, visitors paid a toll to cross the chasm between St Nicholas Cliff and the Spa. In this view, the iron footbridge frames the Rotunda Museum, another distinctive structure.

Hold your horses

The White Horse of Kilburn, a fixture on Roulston Scar since 1857, can be seen twenty-eight miles (45km) away. Chalk was used by Kilburn schoolmaster John Hodgson, his pupils and local volunteers to create the horse, which is 318 feet (97m) long and 220 feet (67m) high.

Left: Very few people are lucky enough to get this view of the White Horse. Here's how it looks from the air.

Middle: Seen from Byland, the White Horse stands out sharply amid the russets and golds of autumn.

Right: High summer in Kilburn, and Roulston Scar's famous embellishment contrasts sharply with the surrounding foliage.

The way through the woods

Left: A carpet of wild garlic adds a splash of colour – and a nostril-tweaking aroma – to Robin Hood's Howl, a beauty spot a mile (1.5km) west of Kirkbymoorside. Howl means hole or hollow.

Top Right: Autumn shades at Rievaulx in the valley of the Rye. The fingerpost invites the walker to make for the neighbouring town of Helmsley.

Bottom Right: One of the caves to be found in Little Beck Wood, a 64-acre (26ha) nature reserve containing oak trees up to 200 years old.

A fond farewell

Top Left: The Esk estuary and Whitby's rooftops bask in the bewitching glow of the setting sun.

Bottom Left: The North York Moors are peppered with standing stones. This example is on Blakey Ridge, the high ground separating Rosedale and Farndale.

Right: The dying embers of an autumn day at Sutton Bank, with Whitestone Cliff and Gormire Lake increasing the interest rate. Fictional vet James Herriot, created by Thirsk author Alf Wight, described this view as the finest in Britain.

Index

Baysdale, 52
Beck Hole, 7
Bilsdale, 42
Blakey Ridge, 41, 62
Bodley, George Frederick, 49
Boggle Hole, 4, 38
Bransdale, 42
Bridestones, 17
Byland Abbey, 10
Castleton, 30
Castleton Rigg, 41
Cleveland Way, 18
Cook, Captain James, 23, 44
Coxwold, 40
Dalby Forest, 18

Danby Dale, 41, 43
Darnholm, 14
Dungeon Hole, 18
Easby Moor, 45
Easterside Hill, 42
Egton Bridge, 46
Egton Bridge Gooseberry Show, 55
Egton High Moor, 21
Esk, River, 46, 62
Farndale, 41, 62
Fat Betty, 53
Filey, 36
Gisborough Priory, 10
Goathland, 27
Gormire Lake, 17, 63
Great Ayton, 29

Grosmont, 14
Hambleton Hills, 34
Hayburn Wyke, 7
Heartbeat (tv series), 27
Helmsley, 57
Herriot, James, 63
Hole of Horcum, 21
Hood Hill, 34
Huntcliff, 18
Hutton-le-Hole, 28
Lastingham, 29
Lealholm, 46
Leven, River, 29, 56
Little Beck Wood, 61
Lockton, 29

Mallyan Spout, 7
Mount Grace Priory, 13
Newton Dale, 14
North Dale, 14
North Yorkshire Moors Railway, 14
Nunthorpe, 8
Osmotherley, 13
Over Silton, 49
Pickering, 35, 48
Port Mulgrave, 24, 50
Ralph's Cross, 44
Ravenscar, 50
Rievaulx, 61
Rievaulx Abbey, 13
Robin Hood's Bay, 4, 18, 38, 50

Roseberry Topping, 8
Rosedale, 35, 53, 62
Roulston Scar, 58, 59
Runswick Bay, 23, 51
Ryedale Show, 54, 55
Saltburn, 18, 32, 38
Saltwick Bay, 4
Sandsend, 38
Scarborough, 4, 23, 36, 49, 57
Seven, River, 31
Sinnington, 31
Staindale Lake, 18
Staithes, 23, 26
Stokesley, 55, 56
Sutton Bank, 34, 63

Thirsk, 33
Thomason Foss, 7
Upleatham, 48
West Beck, 7
Westerdale, 41, 44, 4
Whitby, 13, 23, 25, 3(
35, 37, 45, 62
White Horse of Kilbu 40, 58, 59
Whitestone Cliff, 63
Vale of York, 40

Photographic Acknowledgements

Marc Bedingfield, p38 top; Lee Beel, (www.lee-beel-photography.co.uk), p53 bottom; Richard Burdon, (www.rjbphotographic.co.uk), pp17, 19, 20, 26, 35 left top & bottom, 37; Chris Ceaser, (www.chrisceaser.com), p4, 5 bottom, 6 left & right, 16, 22 top right, 35 right, 38 bottom left & right, 50, 59, 61 bottom, 62 top & bottom; Alan Curtis, 22 left, 49 bottom right; John Devlin (www.stockimages.co.uk), p53 top; Chris Dyson, (www.chrisdysonphotography.com), p33 top; Terry Foster, p51; Andrew Gallon, pp14, 15; Deryck Hallam, p29 middle; Granville Harris, (www.granvilleharrisphotography.co.uk), p31; Andrew Hopkins, p25; Roger Keech (www.rkstills.co.uk), 58 left; Mike Kipling, (www.mikekiplingstockphotos.co.uk), pp7, 8, 9, 11, 13 bottom, 21, 22 bottom right, 23, 24, 27, 28, 29 left, 30, 33 bottom, 34, 36 left & right, 41 top & bottom, 43, 44 left, 45, 47, 48 left, 49 top, 50 bottom, 55 left top & bottom, 56 57, 59, 63; Andy Latham, (www.andylatham.co.uk), p18 botto John Potter, (www.jpotter-landscape-photographer.com), pp40, 54, right, 61 top; Ian Snowdon, 18 top, 39, 45; Mark Sunderland, (w marksunderland.com), pp12, 29 right, 48 right, 56 right; Rich Watson (www.richardwatsonlandscapephotography.co.uk), pp13 42 right, 46 top, 52, 60; Graham Wolfenden, p5 top.